Ze

# of Recipes

This is my third book of recipes, which comes as the result of your many requests for a book containing the recipes shown on the BBC Television programmes 'Town and Around', 'Look East', 'South Today', and 'Midlands Today'.

It contains a hundred new recipes. The majority of these have been demonstrated during the past year, up to the end of June this year, when the book went to the printers.

It was not possible to include all the recipes shown in this time as they are too numerous, but I hope you will like my selection. Once again they have been designed, as far as possible, to use foods available in the average home, and I hope you will enjoy them.

My thanks go to the staff of the BBC without whom there would not be a programme, to my family who continue to test the recipes and help in so many ways, my friend who typed all the recipes for this book, and finally to 'you', my many unseen friends who join me every week in the BBC kitchen. To you all I say 'Thank you' and 'Bon Apetit'.

Zena Skinner

Zena Skinner's Third Book of Recipes

drawings by Juliet Renny

British Broadcasting Corporation

Published by the
British Broadcasting Corporation
35 Marylebone High Street
London W.1

First published 1966
Reprinted 1967

Printed and bound in Great Britain by
Hazell Watson & Viney Ltd
Aylesbury, Bucks
No. 6938/2

Contents

FISH

POULTRY AND HARE

PUDDINGS (HOT)

PUDDINGS (COLD)

VEGETABLES AND SALADS

PICNICS AND PARTIES

DRINKS

Cakes and Bread

1. FLORENTINES

Once you have made these I am sure they will become firm favourites with the family.

INGREDIENTS

2 oz. butter
2 oz. castor sugar
1 dessertspoonful golden syrup
2 oz. plain flour
1 oz. chopped blanched almonds
1 oz. chopped candied peel
1 oz. chopped glacé cherries
1 oz. sultanas
1 oz. chopped angelica
1 teaspoonful lemon juice

METHOD: Well grease several large baking tins. In a saucepan melt the butter, sugar and syrup over a low heat; when melted stir in the flour, fruit and nuts, finally adding the lemon juice. Once the ingredients are evenly blended, drop teaspoonsful of the mixture on to the baking sheets, allowing approximately 4 to a sheet as they spread during cooking. Bake at approximately 325° F or mark 2–3 for about 10 minutes or until golden brown. Remove the tins from the oven, leave the florentines on them for 2 minutes, then remove with a palette knife. Place them on cooling trays to get quite cold, then spread the smooth side with melted dark chocolate, marking a pattern with a fork. Allow the chocolate to set, then store them in an airtight tin.
N.B. 2 oz. of chocolate melted in a basin over a pan of hot water should be enough to cover the base of the florentines.

(Approx. 24)

2. CHOCOLATE FRUIT AND NUT CAKE

If you don't like raisins here's a fruit cake without any. A nice cake to make for Mothering Sunday.

INGREDIENTS

6 oz. butter
6 oz. castor sugar
Grated rind of 1 large orange
3 large eggs
8 oz. plain flour
1 oz. cocoa powder
1 level teaspoonful baking powder
6 oz. sultanas
6 oz. currants
4 oz. chopped blanched almonds

METHOD: Grease and line with double greaseproof paper a 7½" round cake tin. In a basin cream the butter, sugar and orange rind until light and fluffy. Gradually add the beaten eggs with a tablespoon of sifted flour. Sieve the remaining flour, baking powder and cocoa together into the mixture and add the fruit and nuts. Stir all together until evenly blended, then turn the mixture into the prepared tin. Bake at approximately 325° F or mark 2 for about 1¾ hours. To test when done insert a steel knitting needle into the centre of the cake two or three times. If the needle comes out clean, the cake is done. Store in an airtight tin until required. (7½" round cake)

3. BUFTON SQUARES

This recipe was given to me by a friend when I visited her kitchen one day.

INGREDIENTS

4 oz. plain flour
Small pinch salt
1 oz. semolina
4 oz. rolled oats
1 level teaspoonful bicarbonate of soda
2 level teaspoonsful baking powder
1 tablespoonful warm water
1 oz. golden syrup
4 oz. castor sugar
5 oz. margarine
1 oz. chopped blanched almonds
1 oz. chopped glacé cherries

METHOD: In a basin mix together the flour, salt, semolina, oats and bicarbonate of soda. Dissolve the baking powder in the water. In a saucepan dissolve the syrup, sugar and margarine, and when melted add to the dry ingredients. Next add the baking powder and water, and finally the cherries and almonds. Mix all well together and spread into a large well-greased swiss roll tin. Bake at approximately 350° F or mark 3 for 20–30 minutes, when the top will be firm.

(Approx. 18 portions)

4. BONFIRE CAKE

A no-bake cake for the children after the fireworks!

INGREDIENTS

8 oz. Rich Tea biscuits
4 oz. Digestive biscuits
4½ oz. butter
1½ oz. castor sugar
4½ level tablespoonsful clear honey
1½ oz. cocoa
6 oz. California seedless raisins (chopped)

METHOD: Crush the biscuits very finely. In a basin cream the butter and sugar until light and fluffy, add the honey and cocoa and continue creaming until evenly blended. Blend in the biscuit crumbs and raisins. Press the mixture into one 9″ straight-sided sandwich tin which has been lightly greased *or* two 6″ sandwich tins. The mixture must be really well pressed down until the surface is even and firm. Leave to set overnight.

Ice the cake by spreading butter icing all over, and this is made by blending 2 oz. of butter and 4 oz. of icing sugar together. Decorate with barley sugar sticks, piled on top, and some red and gold flames cut out from red and gold paper.

(6″ round cake)

5. PLAIN AND CHOCOLATE SPONGE CAKES

Chocolate and plain sponge cakes for parties, with several variations for filling and icing.

Plain Sponge

INGREDIENTS

3 standard eggs
4 oz. castor sugar
5 oz. self-raising flour
Few drops fresh lemon juice

Chocolate Sponge

INGREDIENTS

3 standard eggs
3 oz. castor sugar
3 oz. plain flour
1 level tablespoonful cocoa

METHOD: (Both cakes) Grease and dust with flour two 7″ sponge sandwich tins. In a basin whisk the eggs and sugar together until thick and creamy. The mixture should leave a distinct trail across the surface when the beater is lifted up. Fold in the sieved flour *or* flour and cocoa until evenly blended.

Divide the mixture evenly between the tins and bake at approximately 425° F or mark 8 (*for plain sponge*) 12–15 minutes, and for (*chocolate sponge*) 10–12 minutes.

6. FILLINGS FOR SPONGE CAKES

Filling and Icing for Chocolate Sponge

INGREDIENTS

4 oz. butter
8 oz. icing sugar
1 teaspoonful coffee essence
¼ lb. chocolate peppermint creams

METHOD: In a basin cream half of the butter and half of the icing sugar together; when soft and fluffy add the essence and mix well. Spread this mixture in the centre of the sponge as the filling. Cream the remaining butter and sugar together in the same way, and pipe it on the top of the sponge in circles, alternating the circles with a ring of peppermint creams.

Filling and Icing for Plain Sponge (1)

INGREDIENTS

2 oz. butter
3 oz. icing sugar
2 level tablespoonsful lemon curd
3 oz. butter
6 oz. icing sugar
4 oz. toasted almonds
3–4 orange and lemon slices

METHOD: Cream the 2 oz. of butter and 3 oz. of icing sugar together until light and fluffy, add the lemon curd and beat again. Place this filling in the sponge.

Cream the remaining butter and sugar together in the same

way and coat the sides of the sponge, also the top. Roll the cake on its side and coat with the almonds. Place the orange and lemon slices in a pattern on the top.

Filling and Icing for Plain Sponge (2)

INGREDIENTS

3 oz. butter
6 oz. icing sugar
Six 3d. chocolate flakes
8 chocolate buttons

METHOD: Cream the butter and sugar together until light and fluffy, spread two-thirds on the inside of the sponge cakes for the filling, and chop up two of the flakes and put these in the centre of the cake.

Spread the remaining butter cream on the top of the cake and round the outer edge alternate chocolate buttons with the remaining flakes which have been cut in half crosswise. Candles can be added if the event is a birthday.

7. CHRISTMAS SPONGE CAKE

This can ring the changes with the 'traditional' Christmas cake especially liked by children.

INGREDIENTS

Sponge

6 oz. butter or margarine
6 oz. castor sugar
3 large eggs
6 oz. self-raising flour
Few drops vanilla essence
Little strawberry jam (for filling)

Icing

3 oz. butter
6 oz. icing sugar

Decoration

½-lb. packet chocolate finger biscuits
Small Father Christmas

METHOD: Grease and dust with flour two 7″ diameter by 1″ deep sponge sandwich tins. Cream the butter and sugar together until light and fluffy, add the essence and also the eggs one at a time with a tablespoonful of flour. Beat all thoroughly together then fold in the remaining flour. Divide the mixture evenly between the two tins and bake at approximately 375° F or mark 4–5 for about 30–35 minutes. Turn out on to a cooling tray and allow to become quite cold before filling.

To fill the cake beat together the butter and icing sugar until soft and light in colour. Spread the jam on both halves of the cake, sandwich together and then coat the outside and top with the butter icing.

To decorate: Put the finger biscuits round the side of the cake, leaving 6 to decorate the top. Press them firmly into the icing and tie a ribbon round the centre of the biscuits. Place the 6 remaining biscuits on the top and also the Father Christmas.

(12 portions)

8. TOFFEE CRUNCH

Quick and easy to make and very popular, so make plenty.

INGREDIENTS

2 oz. marshmallows
2 oz. toffee (plain)
1 oz. butter
2 oz. rice crispies

METHOD: In a saucepan put the butter, toffee and marshmallows, and allow to melt and blend together on a very low heat. When evenly blended remove from the heat and stir in the rice crispies until they are covered. Place heaps on to a greased baking tin and allow to set. When cold and set, store in an airtight tin. (10–15 portions)

9. BROWN HOME-MADE BREAD

I always find great satisfaction in making home-made bread, and it isn't really as difficult as some people imagine.

INGREDIENTS

3 lb. wholemeal flour
2 oz. fresh yeast or 2 rounded teaspoonsful dried yeast
1 level tablespoonful brown sugar or treacle
4 level teaspoonsful salt
2 pints (approx.) warm milk and water

METHOD: Sieve half the flour into a warm bowl. Mix the warm milk and water, sugar or treacle and yeast in a jug and stir well. Make a batter with the flour and warm yeast liquid, and beat well. Cover the basin and put in a warm place until it froths, approximately 10–15 minutes. Add sufficient of the remaining flour and all the salt to make a soft (scone-like) dough. Knead the dough repeatedly for 5–10 minutes.

Divide the dough into four and shape each quarter into a roll on a floured board. Place in the greased tins (two thirds full), cover with a damp cloth and leave in a warm place to rise to the top of the tins. When well risen, remove the cloth and brush the top of each loaf with a little milk or melted margarine. Bake in a hot oven at approximately 450° F or mark 8 for 30–40 minutes. Test to see if the loaves are baked by rapping the bottom with the knuckles, and if they sound hollow cool on a wire rack. (4 small 1-lb. loaves *or* 2 large 2-lb. loaves)

10. MALTED FRUIT LOAF

A nice moist loaf that will keep for a week or so in a tin. Spread with butter it's delicious for tea.

INGREDIENTS

- 6 oz. dates or raisins (stoned and chopped)
- 1 level teaspoonful bicarbonate of soda
- $\frac{1}{3}$ pint boiling water
- 2 oz. butter or margarine
- 4 oz. castor sugar
- 2 level dessertspoonsful malted milk powder (Horlicks type)
- 1 large egg (beaten)
- 12 oz. self-raising flour
- 1 level teaspoonful baking powder
- 1 drop vanilla essence
- 2 oz. walnuts (chopped)

METHOD: Grease and line the base of a 2 lb. loaf tin with greaseproof paper. Into a basin put the dates and bicarbonate of soda, pour on the boiling water and leave to cool, stirring occasionally. Cream butter, mix sugar and malted milk powder together, add to butter and continue creaming until light and fluffy. Add egg gradually. Sieve flour and baking powder together and gradually add to the creamed mixture alternately with the date mixture. Finally add the vanilla essence and walnuts and mix all well together. Put the mixture into the prepared tin and bake at approximately 325° F or mark 3 for about 1½ hours. Remove from the tin when done and leave to get cold on a cooling tray. Spread with butter and serve.

(Approx. 20 portions)

11. QUICK WHEATMEAL BREAD

This is a quick way of making home-made bread, and the finished loaves certainly justify the effort.

INGREDIENTS

- 12 oz. strong plain white flour
- 12 oz. wholemeal flour
- 3 level teaspoonsful castor sugar
- 3 level teaspoonsful salt
- 1 oz. fresh yeast *or* ½ oz. dried yeast
- ¾ pint luke warm water

METHOD: In a large basin mix together the flours, salt and sugar. Blend the yeast in the water, make a well in the centre of the flour and pour in all the liquid. Mix to a soft, scone-like dough, adding a little extra flour if necessary. When the mixture is thoroughly mixed it should leave the bowl clean. If using dried yeast mix and add to the mixture as directed on the packet.

Divide the dough into two equal pieces, turn them on to a lightly-floured board, and knead with the hands, until it feels firm and elastic and no longer sticky. Mould the dough into shape to exactly fit the tin, and place in the well-greased tin. Mould the second piece in the same way and then put both tins into a polythene bag in a warm place for the dough to rise to the tops of the tins. When risen remove from the bag and bake at approximately 450° F or mark 8 for 30–40 minutes.

To test when cooked – remove the loaf from the tin, tap the base with the knuckles and if it sounds hollow the bread is cooked. Cool on a wire tray. (Two 1-lb. loaves)

To make White Bread use all white flour and make as above.

To make Brown Bread use all wholemeal flour and make as above, using a little extra water if required.

12. SCONE MEAL LOAVES

There was a bread strike on and yeast was short, so this was made to fill the gap.

INGREDIENTS

$1\frac{1}{2}$ lb. brown scone meal (from food health shops)
2 oz. butter or margarine
$\frac{1}{2}$ teaspoonful salt
$\frac{1}{4}$ pint milk
$\frac{1}{2}$ pint water

METHOD: Well grease two 6–7″ sponge sandwich tins. Put the flour into a basin, add the salt and rub in the butter or margarine. When the butter has been rubbed in finely, add all the liquid and mix well together. Turn the dough out on to a lightly-floured board, divide into 2 equal parts, and mould each piece into a round, flattening the top slightly. Put the shaped dough into the prepared tins and bake at approximately 425° F or mark 8 for 25–35 minutes, or until the crust turns golden brown. (Two 6–7″ rounds)

13. CHELSEA BUNS

Yeast cooking is always fun, and your family and friends are sure to enjoy these.

INGREDIENTS

Dough

1 lb. plain flour
1 oz. fresh yeast *or* $\frac{1}{2}$ oz. dried yeast
Large pinch salt
2 oz. melted butter
$2\frac{1}{2}$ oz. castor sugar
$\frac{1}{2}$ pint milk

Filling for $\frac{1}{2}$ dough

$\frac{1}{2}$ oz. melted butter
2 oz. castor sugar
2 oz. currants
1 oz. mixed candied peel
Small pinch mixed spice
} Mix all together

METHOD: Into a basin sieve the flour and salt and add the sugar except for 1 dessertspoonful. Heat the butter and milk together until warm, then add the yeast which has been creamed with the remaining dessertspoonful of sugar, and pour into the flour. Mix to a soft dough and knead with the hand until smooth. Cover the basin with a polythene bag or cloth and place in a warm place to rise to double its size, approximately 1–1½ hours.

When risen, divide the dough in half leaving one half in the basin, and kneading the other half on a lightly floured board. Roll into an oblong and brush with the ½ oz. of melted butter, then sprinkle the fruit and sugar mixture evenly over the surface. Roll up like a swiss roll, and cut into 10 slices. Put these into a greased sandwich tin, cut side down, leaving room for them to rise, *i.e.* 5 slices in a 7″ sandwich tin is sufficient.

Leave to rise for approximately 20–30 minutes in a polythene bag, then bake at approximately 425° F or mark 8 for 15–20 minutes.

To glaze the tops of the buns: Mix 1 dessertspoonful of castor sugar with 1 tablespoonful of cold water, brush the tops of the buns when cooked, and put back into the oven for about 1 minute. Turn out on to a wire cooling tray and separate when cold. (10 buns)

14. DOUGHNUTS

If you start eating them directly they're cooked they won't last very long – so avoid temptation.

INGREDIENTS

½ the dough from the Chelsea bun recipe
Castor sugar and cinnamon for coating
Jam for filling
Fat or oil for deep fat frying

METHOD: Turn the dough on to a lightly floured board, knead well, then divide into equal sized pieces. Shape each piece into a ball then flatten slightly, place a little jam in the centre of each piece and gather up the edges over the jam taking care to seal the jam inside.

Place the doughnuts on floured baking tins, put in a polythene bag and leave to rise in a warm place until they double their size, approximately 10 minutes.

Heat the fat or oil to a cooking temperature, fry the doughnuts until golden brown all over, turning them over during cooking, approximately 5 minutes. Drain well and toss in the cinnamon sugar, until coated all over.

(Approx. 12 doughnuts)

Pastries and Savouries

15. SARDINE EGG AND TOMATO PIE

This was made from ingredients I had in the larder when the shops were shut and friends had arrived.

INGREDIENTS

6 oz. rough puff pastry
4-oz. can sardines in oil
2 hard boiled eggs
3 small tomatoes (skinned and sliced)
Few drops lemon juice

METHOD: Roll out a little under half of the pastry and line a 7–8″ ovenproof plate. Drain the sardines and break up with a fork, then spread over the pastry. Sprinkle on the drops of lemon juice, slice the eggs and lay on top of the sardines and the tomatoes on top of the eggs. Roll out the remaining pastry and cover the pie. Seal the edges, decorate and make two or three slits in the centre of the top. Lightly brush with a little milk and bake at approximately 425° F or mark 8 for about 25–30 minutes. Serve either hot or cold. (6–8 portions)

16. MINTED LAMB IN POTATO CASE

At the time I made this the cost was under 2s. per head, a good choice for mid-week.

INGREDIENTS

¾ lb. minced lean breast of lamb
1 small finely chopped onion
½ oz. dripping or lard
½ oz. plain flour
¼ pint stock or water
1 dessertspoonful finely chopped mint
1 lb. cooked mashed potato

METHOD: Melt the fat in a frying pan and fry the onion. Add the meat and brown lightly. Sprinkle in the flour and mint and stir well, then add the stock. Season to taste and bring to the boil, stirring all the time. Cover the pan with a lid and simmer for about 1 hour or until the meat is tender. In the meantime mash the potatoes and spread into a greased 6–7″ ovenproof dish, and pipe round the edge if desired. Place under the grill for a few minutes to brown, then keep hot.

Once the meat is cooked pour into the potato case, decorate with a sprig of parsley if desired and serve at once.

(2–3 portions)

17. BACON AND CORN FLAN

Can be served either hot or cold, and is therefore an ideal choice for a variety of occasions.

INGREDIENTS

8 oz. short crust pastry
4 oz. sweet corn kernels (drained)
4 oz. cooked minced bacon
2 large eggs
¼ pint milk
1–2 drops tabasco sauce
Pepper to taste
1 oz. finely grated cheese

METHOD: Line a 8″ flan ring with the pastry. In a basin mix together the corn and bacon, then sprinkle this into the flan case. Beat together the eggs, milk, sauce and pepper, then pour into the flan case. Sprinkle the grated cheese all over the top and bake at approximately 400° F or mark 6 for about 35 minutes. When the filling has set, carefully remove the flan ring and return the flan to the oven to brown the outside of the flan case. (4–6 portions)

18. HAM AND PORK PASTIES

I made these from ingredients in my store cupboard, when some unexpected friends arrived.

INGREDIENTS

6 oz. puff or rough puff pastry
Little prepared mustard
7-oz. can Danish chopped ham with pork

METHOD: Roll the pastry out thinly, and cut into 3–3½″ rounds with a pastry cutter, making 12 rounds altogether. Place 6 on a baking tin, then cut the canned meat into 6 even slices. Place one piece of meat on each pastry round, spread with a little mustard, damp round the edge of the pastry and cover with the remaining circles. Press the pastry well together, brush with a little milk or beaten egg and make a small slit in the top of each pasty. Bake at approximately 425° F or mark 8 for 15–20 minutes, when the pastry will be golden brown and crisp. These pasties can be served hot or cold. (6 portions)

19. HAM AND CHEESE WHIZ

These can be made in advance and heated when required, and they save on the washing-up!

INGREDIENTS

8 long soft rolls

Filling

2 oz. grated Cheddar cheese
2 tablespoonsful tomato purée or ketchup
2 oz. sliced cooked ham (chopped)
Salt and pepper to taste

METHOD: Cut the rolls in half lengthwise and toast on the inside. Combine the ingredients for the filling until evenly blended, and put an equal amount of filling into each roll, then sandwich the halves together. Wrap each roll in a piece of aluminium foil, and leave in a cool place until required. Place the foil parcels in the oven to heat through for about 15 minutes at approximately 350° F or mark 4. When ready for eating strip back the foil. (8 portions)

20. EGG IN A JACKET

Approximate cost of this dish is 1s. Good for those who have to watch their budget, and Old Age Pensioners.

INGREDIENTS

1 large hard boiled egg
½ oz. plain flour
½ oz. grated Cheddar cheese
½ teaspoonful mixed herbs
2 oz. fresh white breadcrumbs
1 small egg
Salt and pepper to taste

METHOD: In a basin put the breadcrumbs, cheese, seasoning and herbs. Beat the small egg, add this to the mixture to bind the ingredients together as for a stuffing. Coat the hard boiled egg in flour, brushing off any surplus, then press the herb mixture round the egg, covering it closely, and making sure it is smooth and free from cracks. Fry quickly in deep fat until golden brown all over. Drain on absorbent paper. Serve either hot or cold. It is very nice with salad in season. (1 portion)

21. SAUSAGE KEDGEREE

One way of making two cold sausages into a hot meal for two people.

INGREDIENTS

2 pork sausages (cooked)
¾ oz. butter
6 oz. cooked patna rice
1 hard boiled egg (coarsely chopped)
Salt and pepper
Little cayenne pepper
Small pinch grated nutmeg

METHOD: Cut each sausage into 6 slices. Melt the butter in a frying pan or heatproof serving dish, then stir in the rice, sausages and hard boiled egg. Season to taste with the salt, pepper, cayenne and nutmeg, and stir gently until the ingredients are thoroughly heated through. If cooked in a frying pan serve in a hot dish, otherwise serve in the dish in which it was cooked. In either case serve at once. (2 portions)

22. EGG AND TOMATO NEST

A quick and easy dish to make and one I think most of the family would enjoy.

INGREDIENTS

1½ lb. mashed potatoes
14-oz. can peeled tomatoes
Salt and pepper
4 standard eggs
Little thyme
Little grated cheese

METHOD: When mashing the potatoes add 1 egg as well as a little milk, butter and seasoning, and beat them until white and fluffy.

Grease a large ovenproof dish, add the mashed potatoes, building up the sides to form a rim. In the centre put the tomatoes, season, and then break the eggs into the tomato. Sprinkle with a little thyme and finally grated cheese. Cover the dish with a piece of foil and bake at approximately 350° F or mark 4 until the eggs have been poached in the tomato juice, about 1 hour if using tomatoes with very little liquid.

(4 portions)

23. STEAK, BACON AND MUSHROOM PIE

A good dish to feed the children with when they are on holiday.

INGREDIENTS

Topping

4 oz. rough puff pastry *or* A small quantity of hot mashed potato

Filling

1 oz. white fat
1 small onion (peeled and chopped)
2 oz. streaky bacon (cut in small pieces)
2 oz. mushrooms (sliced)
¾ lb. stewing steak (cut into ¼″ cubes)
7 fluid oz. stock or tomato juice
1 small teaspoonful dry mustard
Salt and pepper to taste

METHOD: If using pastry roll out and cut a top for the dish. When using mashed potatoes prepare these while the filling is cooking.

In a frying pan melt the fat and cook the onion and bacon for 2–3 minutes. Toss the steak in seasoned flour and add to the pan, frying lightly, then add the mushrooms. After 2–3 minutes add the remaining ingredients and simmer for about 45 minutes or until the meat is tender.

Pour the ingredients into a heatproof pie dish, cover with the pastry lid and bake at approximately 425° F or mark 8 for about 25 minutes.

Alternatively pipe on the mashed potatoes in a pattern, in both cases brush the top with a little milk and make a hole for the steam to escape. (2–3 portions)

24. SAVOURY BACON ROLL

A good filling and appetising dish for a cold day.

INGREDIENTS

8 oz. rough puff pastry
¼ lb. mushrooms (finely chopped)
4 small tomatoes (skinned and finely chopped)
4 rashers of lean bacon
Salt and pepper

METHOD: Remove the rind from the bacon. In a basin mix together the tomatoes and mushrooms with seasoning to taste.

Roll out the pastry into an oblong approximately 12″ × 8″. Lay the rashers of bacon on the pastry, and spread over the savoury mixture. Moisten the outside edge of the pastry, all the way round, roll up like a roly-poly, and seal the ends well.

Place the roll on a baking sheet, make several cuts in the top of the roll to allow the steam to escape. Brush with a little beaten egg and bake at approximately 425° F or mark 8 for about 45 minutes. Serve hot with gravy and extra vegetables if desired. (6 portions)

Meat

25. QUICK LAMB STEW

This dish costs around 1s. per head, but at the same time is very nourishing.

INGREDIENTS

1 lb. scrag of lamb
  (cut into pieces)
Little seasoned flour
1 oz. dripping or lard
$\frac{3}{4}$ pint stock or water
$\frac{1}{4}$ lb. carrots
3 small onions
3 small tomatoes

METHOD: Trim the meat removing any excess fat. Prepare the vegetables. Toss the meat in the seasoned flour, and shake off any surplus. Heat the fat in a frying pan, add the meat and brown slightly. Transfer the meat to a deep ovenproof casserole, add stock, carrots and onions. Cover with a lid and cook at approximately 325° F or mark 2 for about 2 hours. Remove from the oven, correct the seasoning and add the tomatoes. Continue cooking for a further 30 minutes at the same temperature or until the meat and vegetables are tender. Serve with potatoes. (3–4 portions)

26. BEEF OLIVES

These can be made up in advance, but you'll need to have a little spare time.

INGREDIENTS

1 lb. buttock steak
1 oz. butter or dripping
½ pint stock
2 oz. chopped and fried mushrooms
Salt and pepper
Little flour
4–6 oz. veal forcemeat
Mashed potatoes
Few sprigs parsley

METHOD: Remove skin and fat from the meat, and wipe with a damp cloth. Cut into small oblong pieces as near the same size as possible. Beat them out slightly with a rolling pin or butter pat. Spread a little stuffing on to each piece and roll up, then tie them like a parcel with fine string, and coat with flour. Put them into a pan in which you have melted the fat and brown them all over. Lift them out on to a plate and pour off the fat. To the same pan add the stock, seasonings and mushrooms, and when hot add the rolls, and simmer very gently until the meat is tender, about 1 hour.
To serve: Lift the beef olives on to a hot plate and remove the string. Arrange in a pattern on mashed potatoes, and decorate with parsley. Green peas or carrots are suggested as the vegetables with this dish. (3–4 portions)

27. GINGERED COLLAR

A bacon joint as a main course. I like it for a change as a Sunday roast.

INGREDIENTS

4 lb. piece of British collar bacon (rolled and tied)
1 pint ginger beer
2 heaped tablespoonsful ginger marmalade

METHOD: Soak the bacon in cold water for about 6 hours, drain and wash over with clear water. Put the joint into a deep saucepan, which is just large enough to take it, and pour over the ginger beer. Put on a well-fitting lid, bring the liquid almost to the boil, and then set at a simmering heat to cook the joint, allowing 25 minutes to the lb.

Turn the joint once or twice during the cooking, and after the cooking time is completed, lift the joint from the pan and remove the skin. Place the joint in a roasting pan, score the fat with a sharp knife, and spread the marmalade all over the fat. Place in the oven for approximately 15 minutes, or until the top is glazed, at approximately 450° F or mark 8. Serve either hot or cold. (8–10 portions)

28. STUFFED BEST NECK OF LAMB

Delicious served hot or cold.

INGREDIENTS

1½ lb. best neck of lamb, prepared for stuffing

Stuffing

4 oz. fresh white breadcrumbs
2 oz. chopped suet
1 tablespoonful chopped mint
1 teaspoonful dried herbs (optional)
Little grated lemon rind
1 large egg
Salt and pepper to taste

METHOD: Make the stuffing by putting all the ingredients into a basin, except the egg. Beat the egg lightly, add to the other ingredients and bind the stuffing together. Place the stuffing on the inside of the meat, roll up and secure with skewers or string. Roast at approximately 350°–375° F or mark 3–4. Allow 30 minutes to the lb. plus a further 30 minutes. (3 portions)

29. PORK STEW WITH DUMPLINGS

A hock of pork is a reasonable joint of meat and served with dumplings makes a filling meal.

INGREDIENTS

Stew

3–3½ lb. hock of pork
2 large onions
3–4 large carrots
1 small swede or turnip
Salt and pepper
Stock made from the bones

Dumplings

5 oz. self-raising flour
1 oz. lard
2 oz. chopped suet
1 small egg
Pinch salt

METHOD: Get the butcher to saw the hock into 4 pieces, then remove all bones and put on to cook with water to cover them. Trim the skin and any surplus fat from the meat and cut into cubes. Put the meat into a large saucepan and cover with stock, simmer for 45 minutes, before adding the vegetables. Prepare the vegetables and cut all of them into quarters, add to the saucepan and season to taste. Continue cooking slowly until tender.

In the meantime in a basin rub the lard into the flour, add salt and suet and bind together with the beaten egg. Shape into small dumplings, bring the stew to the boil and drop them in for 15 minutes before serving. (4–6 portions)

30. JOLLOF RICE
(or Rice and Meat Stew)

I first tried this dish in Nigeria, where it is eaten almost every day!

INGREDIENTS

1 lb. lean meat (shin of beef or small chicken)
2 oz. cooking oil or cooking fat
6 small onions
Two 5½-oz. tins tomato purée
½ pint water
½ teaspoonful ground pepper
Salt to taste
1 chilli pepper, very finely diced
10 oz. boiled rice

METHOD: Wash the meat or chicken and cut up into small pieces. Melt the oil or fat in a saucepan, and gently fry the chopped onions. Add the meat, water, pepper, salt and chilli and one tin of tomato purée, put on the lid and simmer for about 1½ hours until the meat is tender. In the meantime wash and cook the rice in fast boiling salted water. When the meat is tender add the rice and the remaining tin of tomato purée and cook for a further 10 minutes. Serve at once. The ideal vegetables to serve with this dish are carrots and green beans or carrots and broccoli. (4 portions)

31. GAMMON SLIPPER

The oatmeal gives a nutty flavoured topping to the gammon.

INGREDIENTS

1½–2 lb. gammon slipper
2 small onions
Bay leaf
1 teaspoonful soft brown sugar (pieces)
Small quantity coarse oatmeal

METHOD: Soak the joint for 6 hours or overnight if preferred. Rub the sugar into the meat section of the joint and leave for 20 minutes. Into a saucepan put the joint, onions, bay leaf and enough water to cover the joint, then bring slowly almost to boiling point. Remove any scum as it rises, reduce the heat to *simmering* point, and simmer 25 minutes to the lb. Twenty minutes before the cooking time is completed, take the joint from the saucepan, remove the skin and coat the fat with coarse oatmeal, pressing it well into the fat. Put into an oven, at approximately 425° F or mark 8, until the oatmeal is golden brown – about 30 minutes. (3–4 portions)

32. SPICY LAMB CHOPS

I found this dish a great favourite with the boys in the studio.

INGREDIENTS

2 chump or loin lamb chops (4–6 oz. each)
2 rashers streaky bacon
1 small onion (chopped)
2 small tomatoes (peeled and sliced)
2 oz. mushrooms (quartered)
1 teaspoonful Worcester sauce
¼ pint stock
1½ oz. butter
Salt and pepper to taste

METHOD: In a frying pan melt the butter, add the chops which have been seasoned with pepper and fry lightly on both sides, about 1 minute. Put these into a greased ovenproof casserole. Remove the rinds from the bacon and cut into ½″ strips, add to the frying pan and fry 1 minute, then add the onion and mushrooms, and fry until the onion is transparent. Add the tomatoes and finally the stock and sauce, season to taste and stir until boiling. Allow to simmer for 5 minutes then pour over the meat in the dish. Cover the dish and cook at approximately 350° F or mark 4 for about 25–30 minutes. Serve at once.

(2 portions)

33. BARBECUED SPARERIBS

This dish can also be cooked in the oven if a barbecue is not available!

INGREDIENTS

2–3 lb. of pork spareribs

Sauce

3 fluid oz. salad oil
4 fluid oz. lemon juice
4 fluid oz. white vinegar
2 level tablespoonsful syrup or treacle
1 level tablespoonful salt
1 level teaspoonful tabasco sauce
8 fluid oz. tomato purée (optional)

METHOD: Crack the spareribs down the centre and chine the bone or ask the butcher to do this for you. Lay the ribs in a

seamless tin or in double foil and cook slowly over the hot coals.

Combine the ingredients for the sauce in a saucepan or clean can and bring to the boil. Baste the ribs frequently with the sauce and cook for about 1 hour, or until the meat is tender and browned. (3–4 portions)

34. BEEF STEW

Wide Mouth Vacuum Flask Recipe
(8-oz. size flask)

A useful recipe during a fuel crisis, or to take to work on a cold day.

INGREDIENTS

- 4 oz. stewing steak (cut into ½″ cubes)
- 1 small onion (finely chopped)
- 1 oz. celery (finely chopped)
- 2 oz. carrots (sliced *very thinly*)
- ½ oz. dripping
- Salt and pepper to taste
- 2½ fluid oz. water
- 1 level dessertspoonful cornflour
- 3 dessertspoonsful cold water

METHOD: Fill the vacuum flask with boiling water to heat and sterilise it and put the lid on firmly.

Melt the dripping in a frying pan and when hot add the onion, celery and carrot and gently fry until the onion is pale golden brown. Add the meat and fry briskly for 5 minutes to seal it, then season to taste. Pour in the 2½ fluid oz. of water, bring the ingredients to the boil, cover and continue boiling on a lower heat for 20 minutes. Remove the pan from the heat and stir in the cornflour, which has been blended with the remaining water to a smooth consistency. Bring the stew to the boil again and cook for a further 5 minutes.

Pour the water out of the flask and immediately fill with the piping hot stew. Close securely. The stew will be ready to eat in 3½ hours but may be left in the flask for a longer period if desired *but not exceeding 8 hours.*

If there should be a small gap unfilled at the top of the flask, top up with boiling water before adding the lid, as the flask retains heat better if completely full. (1 portion)

Fish

35. SOUSED SALMON STEAKS

I used Canadian chilled salmon for this dish as the price suited my pocket.

INGREDIENTS

2 chilled salmon steaks ½" thick
¼ pint tarragon or wine vinegar
¼ pint water
2 small bay leaves
4 cloves
4 peppercorns
2 level teaspoonsful sugar
½ teaspoonful salt
Tiny pinch basil

METHOD: Allow the steaks to thaw, then wash and dry them. Put them into a greased ovenproof dish, cover with vinegar and water, finally sprinkle on the remaining ingredients. Cook covered in a moderate oven at approximately 325° F or mark 2 for 20–25 minutes.

To serve, remove the steaks from the liquid and drain. Leave to become quite cold and then serve with salad in season.

(2 portions)

36. HERRINGS WITH MUSTARD CREAM

Herrings with a mustard flavour give a meal man appeal!

INGREDIENTS

- 4 large herrings
- 1 level tablespoonful English mustard
- 1 level tablespoonful tomato purée
- 1 level teaspoonful castor sugar
- 2 tablespoonsful single cream
- Small pinch mixed herbs
- Salt and pepper
- 1 lemon, for garnish
- Little lemon juice

METHOD: Clean, trim and bone the herrings, then wipe with a clean damp cloth. In a basin mix together the mustard, tomato purée, sugar, cream and herbs until evenly blended, then season to taste.

Spread some of the cream on the inside of each fish, roll up from the tail end, and stand each fillet on end in a greased ovenproof dish. Sprinkle on a little lemon juice, cover with a well fitting lid and bake at approximately 350° F or mark 3–4 for 20–30 minutes. Serve each portion with a wedge of lemon.

(4 portions)

37. PRAWN SALAD WITH HOT MAYONNAISE

Hot mayonnaise is a good combination with this chilled salad.

INGREDIENTS

Salad

- 6 oz. prawns (fresh, canned or frozen)
- 1 lettuce
- Few spring onions
- ½ cucumber
- 2 tomatoes
- 2 hard boiled eggs

Mayonnaise

- 2 standard eggs
- 2 tablespoonsful double cream
- 1 tablespoonful French mustard
- 1 tablespoonful olive oil
- 3 dessertspoonsful white vinegar
- 3 level teaspoonsful castor sugar
- Salt and pepper to taste

METHOD: Shred the lettuce, slice the cucumber and eggs, cut the tomatoes into wedges. Put the lettuce into the centre of a serving dish. Arrange the cucumber and hard boiled eggs alternately round the edge of the dish. Put the prawns on to the lettuce and surround with the tomatoes and onions.

To make the mayonnaise: Beat the eggs and stir in all other ingredients. Put the basin over a pan of boiling water, and cook stirring all the time until the mayonnaise is thick and creamy. Serve at once with the chilled prawn salad. (4 portions)

38. GRILLED PLAICE WITH ORANGE BUTTER

The orange butter gives the plaice a delicious flavour.

INGREDIENTS

3 large fillets of plaice
Little oil or melted butter
Salt and pepper to taste
Grilled mushrooms and parsley to garnish

Orange Butter

½ oz. butter
1 small onion (*very finely chopped*)
1 large orange
Few drops white vinegar

METHOD: *To make the orange butter:* In a small saucepan heat the butter, then cook the onion for about 10 minutes without browning. Turn up the heat a little and cook until the onion begins to colour, add the grated rind of half the orange and the juice of the whole orange. Bring rapidly to the boil, then put the pan on one side.

To grill the fish: Lightly grease an ovenproof dish, then lay the fillets in skin side down. Brush with melted butter or oil and season to taste. Place the dish under the grill on medium heat and cook until tender, then increase the heat to brown lightly. (About 10 minutes cooking time in all.)

Keep the fish hot, and then bring the sauce rapidly to the boil. Add a few drops of vinegar to sharpen, stir well together then pour over the fillets.

Garnish the dish with the grilled mushrooms and parsley and serve at once. (3 portions)

39. CREAMED SCAMPI

This is delicious eaten with rye bread, brown bread or hot toast and the lemon wedges on the side.

INGREDIENTS

1 oz. butter	Salt, pepper and paprika pepper
½ lb. scampi	Little lemon juice
Little plain flour	Chopped parsley for garnish
½ pint double cream	3 lemon wedges

METHOD: Melt the butter in a frying pan or shallow fireproof dish. Toss the drained scampi in the flour to coat all over. Fry *very gently* over a low heat, shaking the pan from time to time. Be careful not to overcook the scampi.

When the scampi are cooked, add the cream and cook for a minute or two again over a low heat. Season with salt, pepper and lemon juice, then add a pinch of paprika to give a little colour. Serve in the dish or turn out into a hot serving dish, and sprinkle with chopped parsley. (3 portions)

40. BAKED DOG FISH OR GURNET FILLETS

This dish makes a nice change to fish and chips and is simple to prepare.

INGREDIENTS

3 dog fish or gurnet fillets about 8 oz. each	1 medium sized onion (fried in 1 oz. butter)
1 oz. butter	Salt and pepper
4–5 small tomatoes	1 lemon for garnish

METHOD: Grease an ovenproof dish, and melt the 1 oz. of butter, dip both sides of the fish into the butter, and place in dish. Peel the tomatoes, remove the seeds and cut into dice, also peel and finely chop the onion, then fry lightly in the other 1 oz. of butter. Mix the tomato and onion together, and place down the centre of each fillet or all over if preferred. Season with salt and pepper, and bake covered for about 15 minutes at approximately 425° F or mark 8. Garnish with the lemon and serve at once, with peas or beans and fried potatoes.

(3 portions)

41. ORANGE PICKLED HERRINGS

A good dish for the summer months, and it can be prepared in advance.

INGREDIENTS

4 herrings
1 orange
¼ pint white vinegar
1 small onion or shallot (sliced)
4 peppercorns
2 bay leaves
1 level teaspoonful salt
Mixed green salad and dressing
1 piece aluminium foil

METHOD: Cut the herrings and also remove the heads and backbones. Wash well and drain, then cut each fillet in half and roll them up starting with the head end. Secure the roll by pushing a wooden cocktail stick through the centre.

Place the herrings in a deep casserole, then prepare the pickle. Thinly peel the orange skin and add to the casserole with the vinegar, onion, peppercorns, bay leaves, salt and ¼ pint cold water. Cover the dish with the foil and cook at approximately 350° F or mark 4 for about 30 minutes, or until the fish are tender. Leave the fish to cool in the liquid, then drain well. Serve with the salad, which has been tossed in the dressing of your choice.

N.B. The orange can be squeezed and the juice drunk as a starter to the meal. (4 portions)

42. TROUT WITH ALMOND SAUCE

Whether you catch the trout or buy them, this is a delicious dish.

INGREDIENTS

3 fresh trout
2 oz. plain flour } Seasoned flour
Salt and pepper } Seasoned flour
2 oz. butter
1 dessertspoonful vegetable oil

Sauce

2 oz. butter
1½–2 oz. sliced or split almonds
Juice of 1 lemon
Little black pepper

METHOD: Clean, wash and drain the fish. Coat all over in the seasoned flour. In a large frying pan heat the butter and oil together, and when hot, put the fish in one at a time. Cook approximately 5 minutes, then carefully turn the fish over, taking care not to pierce the flesh. Continue cooking for about another 5 minutes. Lift the fish out, put on to a warm serving dish and keep hot.

Wipe out the frying pan with absorbent paper, then heat the remaining 2 oz. butter, add the almonds and cook until golden brown about 2–3 minutes. Add the lemon juice and black pepper, mix all together, then pour over the trout and serve at once. (3 portions)

43. SWEET PUNGENT PRAWNS

This is a special occasion dish on the expensive side, as it needs 1 lb. of fresh prawns.

INGREDIENTS

- 1 lb. fresh or frozen prawns
- 9-oz. can pineapple rings
- 1½ oz. brown sugar
- 4 fluid oz. white wine (dry type)
- 1 tablespoonful soy sauce
- 1 pint water
- ¾ oz. cornflour
- 1 green pepper (cut into strips)
- 3 small tomatoes (cut into wedges)
- 4 portions cooked rice
- 2–4 oz. blanched and toasted almonds

METHOD: Drain the syrup from the can of pineapple into a saucepan, then add sugar, wine, soy sauce and ¾ pint of water and bring to the boil. In a basin mix the cornflour with the remaining ¼ pint of water, then add to the ingredients in the saucepan. Cook, stirring constantly, until thickened.

Add green pepper, pineapple which has been cut into chunks and tomatoes. Cook for 2 minutes then add the prawns and cook until they are thoroughly heated. Serve at once with the cooked rice, to which has been added the blanched and toasted almonds. (4 portions)

44. FISH CURRY

A taste of curry with fish, using the Indian spices. These can be adjusted to suit individual tastes.

INGREDIENTS

1 lb. filleted cod or similar fish
1½ oz. butter or butter fat (ghee)
2 medium sized tomatoes
1 medium sized onion
2 dessertspoonsful powdered dhania or fresh parsley
1 teaspoonful garam-masala
1 teaspoonful turmeric
1½ teaspoonsful salt
½ teaspoonful chilli powder
1 dessertspoonful desiccated coconut
2 small cloves of garlic
1 tablespoonful fresh lemon juice

METHOD: Into a saucepan put the finely chopped onion, garlic and dhania or parsley and gently fry in the butter or ghee. Next add the turmeric, garam-masala, salt, chilli powder and coconut, mix well and allow to cook for a few minutes. Add the sliced tomatoes and fry until tender, stir in the lemon juice and mix all well together. Cook this mixture gently for 4–5 minutes,

then add the well washed and drained fish which has been cut into pieces, but not too small, and leaving the skin on. Cover the fish very carefully with the sauce, and when it starts to boil cover with a lid and allow the curry to simmer for 7–10 minutes, just until the fish is cooked. Do not let it become soft and mashy. If you prefer a drier curry, remove the lid while it is simmering. Serve with a dish of long grain rice.

(4 portions)

Poultry and Hare

45. CHICKEN WITH ORANGE SAUCE

This has become one of my family's favourite ways of cooking chicken portions.

INGREDIENTS

4 chicken portions
2 oz. crushed cornflakes
½ level teaspoonful ground ginger
½ level teaspoonful salt
Pinch pepper
1 standard egg
Little plain flour
Oil or fat for frying
1 orange (cut into wedges for garnish)

Sauce

Grated rind of 1 orange
1 tablespoonful orange juice
1¼ oz. castor sugar
3 level tablespoonsful red currant jelly

METHOD: On a plate mix the cornflakes, salt, pepper and ginger. Wipe the chicken joints dry, then dip in flour followed by beaten egg. Coat well with the cornflake mixture, and fry over a moderate heat until golden brown and tender about 15–20 minutes. Be sure to turn the joints over after the first 10 minutes of the cooking time.

In a basin beat well together the orange rind, sugar and jelly, finally adding the juice and mixing well together. Serve the chicken garnished with the orange wedges, and the sauce separately. (4 portions)

46. DUCKLING SALAD

INGREDIENTS

- 6 oz. cooked duckling meat (diced)
- 3 oz. finely chopped celery
- 1 large eating apple (cored and chopped)
- 1½ oz. chopped nuts (optional)
- Mayonnaise
- Curry powder to taste

METHOD: In a basin mix together the duckling meat, celery, apple and nuts, then add sufficient mayonnaise to bind the ingredients together. Finally stir in curry powder to taste, also salt and pepper if desired. Chill thoroughly and serve on a bed of lettuce, garnished with tomatoes.

N.B. Cooked gosling can be used instead of duckling if desired. (4 portions)

47. QUICK CHICKEN AND HAM PIE

This recipe is designed to use up the left-overs after the Christmas dinner.

INGREDIENTS

- 8 oz. cooked diced chicken
- 4 oz. cooked diced ham
- 10½-oz. can condensed chicken soup
- ¼ pint single cream
- 1 small packet frozen peas (cooked)
- 1 small packet potato crisps

METHOD: Put the soup into a saucepan, stir in the cream and heat very gently. Add the chicken, ham and peas and continue stirring until thoroughly heated through. Pour the ingredients into a hot serving dish, and sprinkle the crisps over the surface. Serve at once. (4 portions)

48. CELERY CHICKEN

Gentlemen – here is a dish for you. It's simple to make when your wife is out or ill in bed.

INGREDIENTS

3–4 chicken portions
1 oz. butter
$10\frac{1}{2}$-oz. can condensed cream of celery soup
Little chopped parsley
$\frac{1}{4}$ pint milk (approximately $\frac{1}{2}$ a can)
1 dessertspoonful fresh lemon juice
Seasoning to taste

METHOD: Melt the butter in a large, deep ovenproof dish. Wipe the chicken portions and place skin side down in the dish, and pour over the lemon juice. Bake at approximately 400° F or mark 6–7 for 20 minutes, then turn the chicken over and bake a further 30–40 minutes at the same temperature.

Stir the milk into the condensed soup, season to taste and pour over the chicken joints, sprinkle the top with parsley and bake a further 20 minutes covered with a piece of foil. Serve with potatoes baked in their jackets. (3–4 portions)

49. DUCK WITH ORANGE SAUCE

These recipes give a choice of poultry for the Christmas dinner, plus a variety of stuffings for the birds. On page 48 are charts for carving the birds which I hope will help the carver!

INGREDIENTS

1 Lincolnshire duckling ($4\frac{1}{2}$–5 lb. dressed weight)
2 tablespoonsful cold water
3 oranges
Watercress for garnishing

Stuffing

1 lb. onions
2 oz. fresh white breadcrumbs
2 teaspoonsful powdered sage
Salt and pepper to taste

METHOD: *To make the stuffing:* Peel and cut the onions into quarters and drop into a little boiling water. Parboil for 15 minutes, drain well then chop add all other ingredients, and stuff the breast or body of the duckling.

Place a large piece of foil in the roasting pan, lay in the duckling and add the water. Wrap the foil loosely round the duckling and cook at approximately 375° F or mark 4–5 for about 2½ hours, when the leg joints should move easily.

Half an hour before the cooking time is finished, fold back the foil to brown the duckling, and add the juice from two of the oranges, baste once or twice during the remaining time. Garnish with the orange slices cut from the remaining orange, which have been lightly fried in a little butter, and add sprigs of watercress just before serving.

50. GOSLING WITH SAGE, ONION AND WALNUT STUFFING

INGREDIENTS

8-lb. gosling
Little flour (plain)

Stuffing

½ lb. onions (peeled and chopped)
1 teaspoonful powdered sage
4 oz. fresh white breadcrumbs
1½ oz. finely chopped walnuts
1 egg
1½ oz. melted butter
Grated rind half lemon
2 teaspoonsful lemon juice
Salt and pepper to taste

Sauce

20-oz. can gooseberries
½ oz. butter

METHOD: *To make the stuffing:* Put the onions into a saucepan, cover with cold water, bring to the boil and simmer 5 minutes. Drain well in a sieve, pressing out any excess liquid. Mix the onions with the sage, breadcrumbs, walnuts and seasoning. Stir in the beaten egg, butter, lemon rind and juice, and place in the neck and or body of the gosling.

Place a large piece of foil into the roasting pan, lay in the gosling and sprinkle the top with a little flour. Fold the foil loosely round the gosling and cook at approximately 375° F or mark 4–5 allowing 20 minutes to the lb. To test when done, place a small skewer into the leg joint, and if the liquid is pink give it a little longer in the oven. Half an hour before the cooking time is completed, fold back the foil to brown.

To make the sauce: Rub the gooseberries through a sieve,

having first drained off the juice. Put the gooseberries into a small saucepan, add the butter and heat. Serve with the gosling and garnish with watercress.

51. CAPON WITH POTATO AND ONION STUFFING

INGREDIENTS

6–7-lb. capon	Few slices fat bacon
Stuffing	
1 lb. mashed potatoes	1 small egg (beaten)
1 medium sized onion (finely chopped)	1 teaspoonful chopped parsley
	Salt and pepper to taste

METHOD: *To make the stuffing:* Mix together in a basin the potato, onion and chopped parsley. Bind to a moist consistency with the egg, and add the seasoning to taste. Place the stuffing into the bird and then put it into the roasting pan in which you require a large piece of foil. Fold the foil loosely round the bird and cook at approximately 325° F or mark 2 for about 2½–3 hours. The slices of bacon should be put over the breast of the bird before closing the foil. To test when cooked the leg joints should move freely and no pink liquid should be visible when a skewer is placed into them. Half an hour before cooking time is finished remove the bacon from the breast and fold the foil back to brown the bird.

52. TURKEY WITH CORN AND CHESTNUT STUFFING

INGREDIENTS

12–14-lb. turkey	Few slices of fat bacon
Stuffing	
12-oz. can chestnut purée	1 lb. sausage meat
11-oz. can giant corn niblets	1 tablespoonful chopped parsley
6 oz. fresh white breadcrumbs	Salt and pepper to taste
4 oz. dripping	

METHOD: *To make the stuffing:* In a basin break the chestnut purée down with a fork, add the drained corn, breadcrumbs, sausage meat, parsley and seasoning, finally binding all together with the melted dripping. Stuff the neck and body of the turkey.

Place a large piece of foil in the roasting pan, put in the bird, add the bacon to the breast and fold the foil loosely round the bird. Cook at approximately 325° F or mark 2 for about 4½–5 hours, and test when done in the same way as given for the capon. Half an hour before the cooking time is finished remove the bacon, fold back the foil to brown the bird.

53. CHICKEN WITH FARMHOUSE STUFFING

INGREDIENTS

4¾-lb. chicken
2–3 slices fat bacon
Bacon rolls for garnish

Stuffing

1½ oz. butter
1 tablespoonful chopped onion
2 rashers chopped streaky bacon
3 oz. fresh white breadcrumbs
Grated rind of half a lemon
2 heaped teaspoonsful chopped parsley
Pinch thyme
Small pinch nutmeg (grated)
Salt and pepper to taste
Little milk

METHOD: *To make the stuffing:* In a small frying pan melt the butter, add onion and bacon and gently fry for several minutes, add the breadcrumbs and cook for a further minute. Add all the remaining ingredients except the milk, and if the consistency is a little dry add some milk. Fill loosely into the neck end of the bird.

Place a large piece of foil into the roasting pan and lay in the chicken, place the bacon slices over the breast of the bird and wrap the foil loosely round. Cook at approximately 375° F or mark 4–5 allowing 20 minutes to the lb. Half an hour before the cooking time is finished, fold back the foil to brown the bird. Serve with grilled bacon rolls.

TURKEY

TURKEY LEG

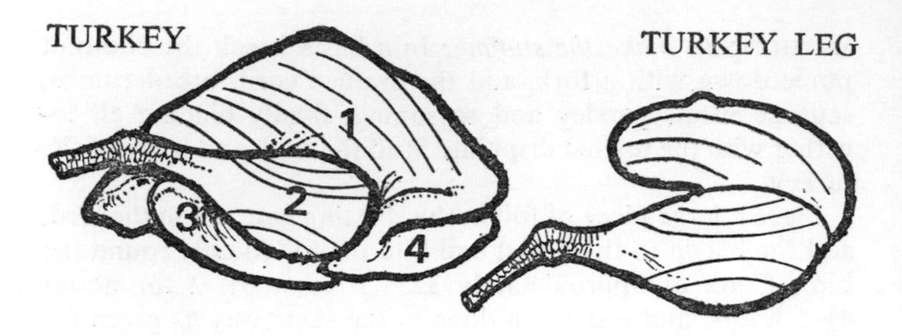

The leg of turkey 2, should not be taken away unless the bird is to be eaten at one sitting. Starting at the leg end of the breast, (1) slice the breast. Serving: slices from the breast and from the drum-stick. Then carve meat from the thigh (3), working up to the wing at (4). Use one side, then the other.

The best way to carve the turkey leg is illustrated by the lines.

CHICKEN

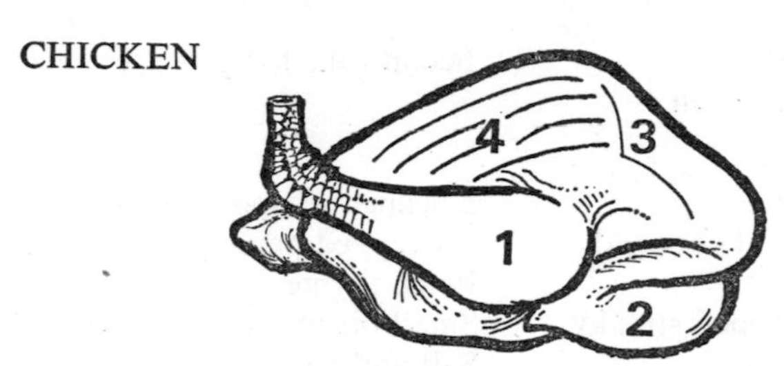

First remove the leg at (1). Now carve the wing at (2). Take out the wish-bone at (3). Then slice the breast at (4).

DUCK

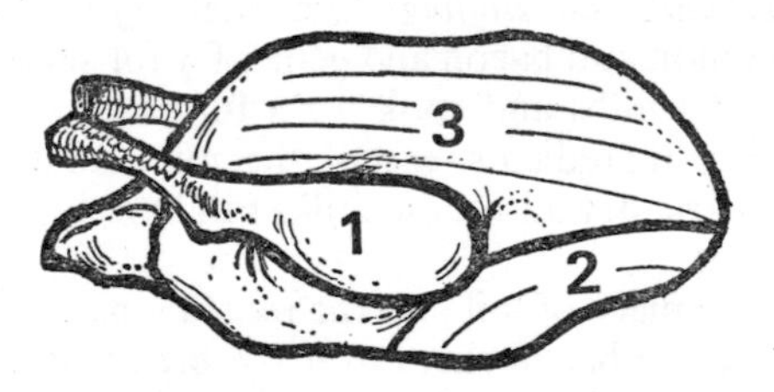

First remove leg at (1) and wing at (2). Then working upwards slice the breast at (3). It is helpful if the wish-bone is removed before cooking.

54. MOTHER'S JUGGED HARE

If you haven't a hare a rabbit will do! Either way it is a delicious main course.

INGREDIENTS

1 small hare (jointed)
Approx. 2 oz. dripping for frying
2–4 oz. flour seasoned with salt and pepper
1 medium sized onion
4 cloves
1 bouquet garni
1–2 wineglasses port wine
Approx. 1 pint stock

METHOD: Wipe the joints with a clean damp cloth, and coat in seasoned flour. In a frying pan heat the dripping and fry the joints until they are well browned all over. Place the joints when fried into a deep casserole, add onion which has been peeled, cut in half and stuck with cloves, and bouquet garni. Put any remaining flour into the frying pan and cook until it browns, then slowly add the stock stirring until it thickens. Pour the stock into the casserole, and if required add a little extra stock to cover the joints. Put on the lid and cook at approximately 300° F or mark 1 until tender, about 2–2½ hours.

Half an hour before serving, remove the onion and bouquet garni and add the port wine. Serve with redcurrant jelly.

(6–8 portions)

Puddings (hot)

55. ALMOND AND MARMALADE PUDDING

A layered pudding with a delicious combination when served hot.

INGREDIENTS

4 oz. butter or margarine
4 oz. dark soft brown sugar (pieces)
2 oz. self-raising flour
1½–2 oz. ground almonds
2 standard eggs
3 level tablespoonsful orange marmalade
Grated rind 1 lemon

METHOD: Lightly grease a pie dish. In a basin cream the butter and sugar until soft. Add the eggs one at a time with a little sieved flour, and the ground almonds. Finally add the lemon rind.

Put approximately half the mixture into the pie dish, spoon the marmalade all over the surface, then cover with the remaining pudding mixture. Cover with a buttered paper and bake at approximately 375° F or mark 5 for about 45–55 minutes. (3–4 portions)

56. BAKED PEACHES

Served hot with whipped cream or ice cream or cold with whipped cream, they are delicious.

INGREDIENTS

4 fresh South African peaches
8 cloves
2 fluid oz. water
3½ oz. castor sugar
¼ oz. butter
Grated rind of half lemon
Whipped cream or ice cream for serving

METHOD: Peel the peaches by dipping them into boiling water. Stick two cloves into each peach and place them into an oven-proof casserole. Combine the sugar and water together and pour over the peaches. Dot the top of the peaches with the butter and sprinkle the grated rind over the top. Cover with a lid and bake at approximately 325° F or mark 2 until tender, about 30 minutes. (4 portions)

57. RHUBARB ORANGE CRUMBLE

This is a variation on the familiar crumble mixture. Rhubarb and orange make it an unusual dish.

INGREDIENTS

1 lb. early rhubarb
1 level tablespoonful golden syrup
Juice of 1 medium sized orange
3 oz. demerara sugar

Crumble

4 oz. self-raising flour
2 oz. butter
1 oz. demerara sugar
Grated rind of 1 orange

METHOD: Cut the rhubarb into ¼" slices and place in a greased 1½–2 pint ovenproof dish. In a saucepan heat together the syrup, orange juice and sugar until evenly blended, then pour this over the rhubarb.

To make the crumble: Sieve the flour, then rub the butter into it until the mixture resembles fine breadcrumbs, stir in the sugar and orange rind. Sprinkle this mixture over the rhubarb, level the top and bake at approximately 400° F or mark 6 for about 35 minutes when the rhubarb should be tender and the top golden brown. (5–6 portions)

58. FRUIT AND NUT PUDDING

A dish for vegetarians and people liking a change in their diet.

INGREDIENTS

1¼ lb. cooking apples (peeled and sliced)
1 oz. raisins
2–3 oz. brown sugar, or to taste
4 oz. margarine
4 oz. brown sugar (pieces)
2 standard eggs
2 oz. ground hazelnuts or almonds
2 oz. wholemeal flour

METHOD: In a saucepan put the peeled, cored and sliced apples, raisins and 2–3 oz. of sugar, and cook gently adding a few drops of lemon juice and 1 tablespoonful of water. When almost cooked, put into a greased 1½-pint pie dish and allow to cool.

In a basin cream together the butter and remaining sugar until light and fluffy, gradually add the eggs and a little flour and when evenly blended fold in the remaining flour and nuts. Spread this mixture over the cooked ingredients and bake at approximately 425° F or mark 8 for about 35 minutes or when the top feels firm to the touch. Serve with custard.

(4–6 portions)

59. SPICED PLUM COBBLER

The 'cobbler' gives a crisp topping to the fresh fruit base.

INGREDIENTS

1 lb. fresh plums
3–4 oz. demerara sugar
¼ level teaspoonful mixed spice

Cobbler

4 oz. self-raising flour
2 oz. butter or margarine
1 oz. castor sugar
Milk to mix
Small quantity milk and sugar to coat

METHOD: Place the plums, which have been washed, cut in half and stones removed, into a 1 pint ovenproof basin. Sprinkle with sugar and spice, and cook covered for 15 minutes at approximately 375° F or mark 5.

To make the cobbler: In a basin sieve the flour and rub in the fat until it resembles fine breadcrumbs, then add sugar and mix to a soft dough with a little milk. Roll out mixture to about ½″ thickness, cut into rounds with 1½″ fluted cutter. Place the rounds slightly overlapping on top of the plums, brush with milk and sprinkle with sugar. Continue baking for 30–35 minutes at approximately 375° F or mark 5.

(2–3 portions)

60. LEMON SNOW

Light-as-air dessert with a tangy lemon flavour. Eat as soon as cooked.

INGREDIENTS

2 oz. butter	1 oz. plain flour
4 oz. castor sugar	Rind and juice of 1 lemon
2 standard eggs	¼ pint milk

METHOD: Grease a 1½ pint ovenproof dish. In a basin cream the butter then add the sugar and beat again until light and fluffy. Add the yolks of the eggs and beat well, then stir in the flour, lemon rind and juice, finally adding the milk. (At this stage the mixture will curdle, but this is quite correct.)

Whisk the egg whites until stiff then fold them into the lemon mixture, when evenly blended pour them into the prepared dish. Stand the dish in a shallow pan of warm water and bake at approximately 350° F or mark 4 for about 35–45 minutes, when the top should be a light golden brown. Serve hot.

(4 portions)

61. CRUNCHY TOPPED APPLE PUDDING

When you're cold and hungry, this is the pudding to have as it is very tasty and filling.

INGREDIENTS

Suet Crust Pastry:
- 6 oz. self-raising flour
- 3 oz. suet
- Pinch of salt
- Cold water to mix

- 1 lb. cooking apples
- Rind and juice of ½ a large orange
- Castor sugar to taste
- 2 tablespoonsful warmed golden syrup
- Approx. 2 oz. demerara sugar

METHOD: Peel, core and slice or chop the apples, and put them into a greased deep pie dish, adding sugar to taste between the layers. Pour over the rind and juice of the orange, and a little more sugar if required.

Make the suet crust pastry by putting all the dry ingredients into a basin and mix to a soft but not sticky consistency. Turn out on to a lightly floured board and press or roll into shape to fit the pie dish. Place the pastry on top of the apples and press down lightly.

With a spoon cover the top of the pastry with the warmed syrup, and lightly press the sugar all over the surface of the syrup. Bake at approximately 350° F or mark 4–5 for about 40 minutes, when the top will be rich golden brown.

(4–6 portions)

62. OATY BLACKCURRANT PUDDING

A variation on a flapjack mixture, combined with blackcurrants, makes this a tasty pudding.

INGREDIENTS

½ lb. blackcurrants
Sugar to taste
4 cloves
⅛ pint water
6 oz. porridge oats
3 oz. butter
2 oz. soft brown sugar (pieces)
1 large egg (lightly beaten)

METHOD: Cook the blackcurrants in ⅛ pint of water, together with the sugar and cloves until soft, then remove the cloves. In a saucepan melt the butter and stir in the brown sugar and oats, finally adding the beaten egg. When all mixed well together put half the oat mixture into a greased pie dish and spread evenly. Next add the blackcurrants and spread over evenly. Finally top with the remaining oat mixture, and cook at approximately 350° F or mark 4 for about 35 minutes when the top will be crisp to the touch. (3–4 portions)

63. WAFFLES AND FRITTERS

These are simple to make if you follow the rules for cooking carefully. They are also delicious at almost any time.

INGREDIENTS

4 oz. self-raising flour	1 large egg
¾ pint cold water	

METHOD: Sieve the flour into a small basin, add the egg and beat the mixture well, gradually adding the water at the same time.

To cook: Heat some fat or oil in a frying pan, placing the waffle iron in the fat as soon as you start to heat the fat. When the fat is hot lower the waffle iron carefully into the batter taking care that the batter does not come over the top of the iron. (A good test as to when the fat is hot enough is when the iron is lowered into the batter it should sizzle.) When the sizzling stops put the waffle into the hot fat, leave for a few seconds, then remove the iron and turn the waffle over. Cook until they are golden brown on both sides. Drain on absorbent paper and serve piping hot with butter and syrup.

Fritters: Using the same batter make them in the same way except when it is cooked on one side, place the filling on top, cover with a second uncooked waffle, and press down gently to seal them together. Turn over to complete the cooking.

Suggested fillings for the fritters: Sliced canned meat, sliced banana, apple rings, lightly cooked bacon, etc.

(Approximately 20 waffles *or* 10 fritters)

64. FRIED BANANA HORNS

Crisply fried pastry with a creamy banana filling.

INGREDIENTS

8 oz. rough puff pastry	Small quantity red currant jelly
4 bananas	Lard or oil for deep fat frying
Small quantity cinnamon and castor sugar	

METHOD: Roll out the pastry to about ⅛″ thickness and cut into 4″ squares. Peel the bananas and cut in half crosswise. Place half banana diagonally in centre of each square. Brush with jelly or toss in cinnamon and sugar which have been mixed together. Brush edges of pastry with a little cold water, and starting with one corner roll up and press seams well together. Fry in the hot fat or oil for about 2 minutes until crisp and golden brown. Drain on absorbent kitchen paper and serve hot sprinkled with castor sugar. (6–8 portions)

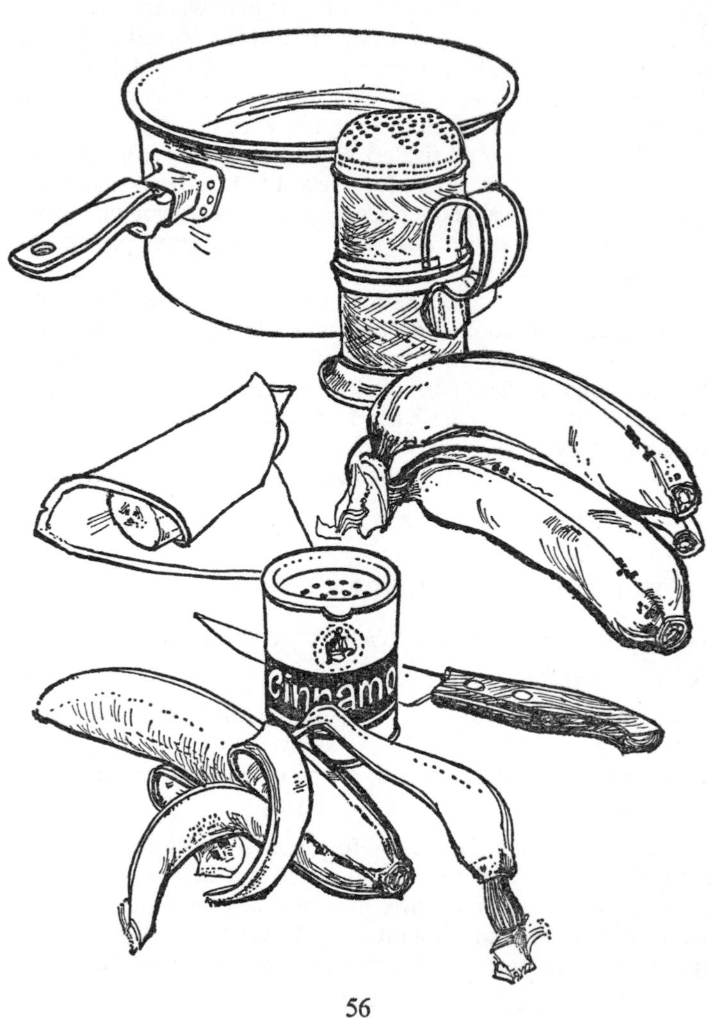

Puddings (cold)

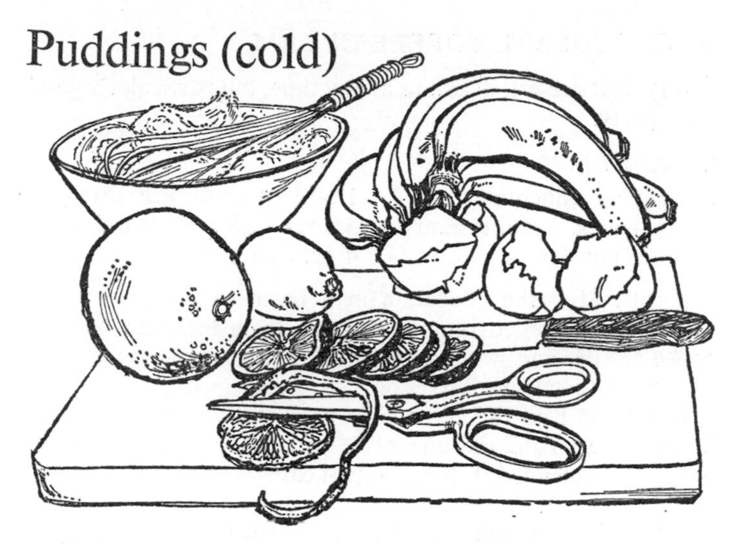

65. BANANA AND ORANGE MERINGUE

Bananas and oranges are always around, so this dessert can be made at any time!

INGREDIENTS

5 ripe firm bananas
2 oranges
Approx. 2½ oz. demerara sugar
2 egg whites
2 level tablespoonsful castor sugar
1 dessertspoonful lemon juice

METHOD: Lightly butter a shallow ovenproof dish, and sprinkle evenly with 1 oz. of the demerara sugar. Peel the bananas, then cut in half lengthwise and crosswise, and arrange on top of the sugar. Sprinkle the bananas with the grated rind of both oranges. Cut the oranges into fairly thin slices, and remove the skin with a pair of kitchen scissors, place these on top of the bananas.

Sprinkle on the remaining 1½ oz. demerara sugar, and the lemon juice. Beat the egg whites until very stiff, then gradually fold in the castor sugar, pile roughly over the fruit and bake at approximately 350° F or mark 3–4 for 15–20 minutes, when the top of the meringue will be nicely browned.

Serve hot or cold, with cream, if desired. (4–6 portions)

66. CHOCOLATE COFFEE CREAM

A very light dessert, delicious at any time, but particularly good for a party.

INGREDIENTS

- 3½ oz. plain chocolate
- 3 level teaspoonsful instant coffee powder
- 1 tablespoonful *warm* water
- 4 large eggs (whites only)
- 4 oz. castor sugar

METHOD: Melt the chocolate in a basin over a pan of hot water. When melted remove the pan from the heat, add the coffee powder and water and stir all the time until the mixture is smooth, then leave it to cool.

In a basin beat the egg whites until stiff and carefully fold in the sugar. Add the chocolate mixture gradually and stir until evenly blended. Fill individual cases with the mixture and chill.

Just before serving top each dish with a little whipped cream or a tiny meringue. (6–8 portions)

67. APPLE CREAM PUDDING

This is pretty enough when made, to serve when guests are expected.

INGREDIENTS

- 4-oz. packet boudoir biscuits
- 1 lb. eating apples (Worcester pearmain)
- ½ pint syrup (½ pint water and 4 oz. castor sugar)
- 1 dessertspoonful fresh lemon juice
- ½ oz. cornflour
- 2–3 tablespoonsful double cream
- 1 large egg (yolk only)
- ½–1 oz. castor sugar
- 1 eating apple cut into slices for garnishing

METHOD: Cut approximately 1″ off each boudoir biscuit and crush the smaller pieces into crumbs. Peel, core and slice the pound of apples, poach in the syrup with a thinly cut slice of lemon until just tender, but not broken. Drain the apples well and leave to cool slightly.

To make the cream filling: In a saucepan put the cornflour, then gradually stir in 6 fluid oz. of the apple syrup, bring to simmering point and *simmer* for 1–2 minutes until the mixture thickens. Remove the pan from the heat and stir in the egg yolk and cream which have been beaten together. Add the lemon rind and juice and sugar to taste.
To assemble the dish: Place half of the apples into a 1 pint straight-sided soufflé dish, stand the boudoir biscuits cut side down, round the outer edge, leaving a small space between each. Pour on half of the cream mixture, then continue with the apples and remaining cream mixture.

Just before serving sprinkle the top with the crumbs, and decorate between each biscuit with a thin slice of the remaining apple. (4–6 portions)

68. FRUIT AND NUT SALAD

A refreshing salad using up the fruit and nuts left over from the holiday.

INGREDIENTS

3 tangerines
1 grapefruit
Juice of 1 orange
2 fresh peaches
2 bananas
2 eating apples
2½ oz. mixed nuts
4 oz. black grapes

Syrup

2 oz. castor sugar
¼ pint water
Juice of ½ lemon

METHOD: Remove the peel, pith and pips from the tangerines and grapefruit, and slice into a serving dish. Make the syrup by heating together all the ingredients until the sugar has dissolved, then allow to get cold.

Add the orange juice to the dish, peel and slice the peaches and put these together with the sliced bananas and peeled and sliced apples. Once they have been coated in the syrup add all to the serving dish. De-seed the grapes and add to dish, and gently mix all the fruits well together.

Just before serving add the nuts and again mix until evenly blended. (4–6 portions)

69. ORANGE AND LEMON PIE

The only cooking with this dish is in melting the margarine. It's quickly made but needs two hours to chill.

INGREDIENTS

Pie Crust

4 oz. digestive biscuits (crushed)
2 oz. margarine
1 oz. castor sugar

Filling

3-oz. packet cream cheese spread
1 small size can condensed milk
1 fluid oz. fresh orange juice
3 fluid oz. fresh lemon juice

METHOD: In a saucepan melt the margarine, remove the pan from the heat and add the sugar and crumbs mixing all well together. Grease a 7″ deep pie plate, put in the crumb mixture and press well down on the base and round the edge. Set aside to harden.

To make the filling: Put the cream cheese into a basin and beat until soft and smooth. Gradually add the condensed milk and juices, and beat until thoroughly blended. Pour the mixture into the prepared crust and chill until set. Decorate as desired or serve with whipped cream. (6 portions)

70. RHUBARB AND GINGER MOUSSE

A recipe which can be made in advance, when rhubarb is in season.

INGREDIENTS

½ lb. rhubarb
Approx. 3 oz. castor sugar
½–1 level tablespoonful chopped ginger
¼ oz. powdered gelatine
2 tablespoonsful cold water
⅛ pint double cream
Few drops red colouring
Whipped cream for decoration

METHOD: Cut the rhubarb into 1″ lengths and stew *very slowly* with the sugar until tender. Add chopped ginger. Put the gelatine in a basin, soften with the water for about 5 minutes, then place basin over a pan of hot water until gelatine is dissolved. Add to the rhubarb mixture and allow to cool.

Whip the cream and gently fold into the rhubarb mixture, then turn into individual serving dishes and decorate with whipped cream if desired. (3 portions)

71. LEMON APPLE CHARLOTTE

A quickly made dessert, but it must be chilled before serving.

INGREDIENTS

1 large cooking apple (peeled and sliced)
Approx. 2 oz. castor sugar
3 level tablespoonsful lemon cheese
4 oz. fresh white breadcrumbs
2 oz. butter

METHOD: Cook the apple and sugar together *very slowly* until the apple is tender, then allow to cool.

Melt the butter in a frying pan, add the breadcrumbs and fry until golden brown, turning constantly.

Into a serving dish put a layer of apple, spread over some lemon cheese, then a layer of crumbs, continue with two further layers of each ingredient, finishing with a layer of crumbs. Chill for 1 hour before serving, and serve with whipped cream if desired. (2–3 portions)

72. MERINGUED ORTANIQUES

Ortaniques are a cross between an orange and tangerine, and when in season ring the changes!

INGREDIENTS

4 large ortaniques
2 egg whites
2 level tablespoonsful castor sugar
2 small ice cream bricks (wafer size)

METHOD: Cut the top off the ortaniques, cut round the segments with a small sharp knife or small pair of scissors, then scoop out the pulp. Remove as much pith as possible without cutting through the shell. Drain excess juice from the fruit, then put fruit back into shells. Whisk the egg whites until stiff, carefully fold in the sugar until evenly blended. Just before serving spoon the ice cream into the shells, and swirl the meringue over the top taking care to cover the ice cream completely.

Cook in the oven at approximately 425° F or mark 8 for 2–3 minutes, just until the meringue is tinged golden brown. Serve at once. (4 portions)

73. BAKED CUSTARD

This recipe tells you how to keep the pastry at the base of the dish.

INGREDIENTS

½ lb. rough puff or short crust pastry	2 large eggs
	1½ oz. castor sugar
1 pint milk	Little grated nutmeg

METHOD: Roll out the pastry and line a deep ovenproof pie-dish. Put the milk and sugar into a saucepan and bring to the boil, remove from the heat and allow to cool slightly. In the meantime beat the eggs lightly together. Once the milk has cooled, pour this on to the eggs whisking all the time, then pour into the lined pie dish. Bake at approximately 400° F or mark 6 for about 10 minutes to brown the crust, then reduce the heat to approximately 300° F or mark 1 for a further 1–1¼ hours or until the custard is set.

N.B. A little grated nutmeg may be sprinkled on top of the custard before baking if liked. For a coffee flavour, add approximately 1 tablespoonful coffee essence or to suit taste. For a chocolate flavour add approximately 1½ tablespoonsful of chocolate powder and ¼ teaspoonful vanilla essence.

(4–6 portions)

74. APPLE AND STRAWBERRY FLAN

Make the flan in advance and prepare other ingredients. It takes about 3 minutes to assemble.

INGREDIENTS

7″ cooked sponge flan
1 lb. cooking apples
¼ lb. fresh strawberries
Few drops of kirsch or orange juice
Small quantity sugar and water

METHOD: Cook the apples in *very little* water until pulped then add sugar to taste, and allow the mixture to become quite cold. Fill the flan with the apple, then top with a layer of whole strawberries which have been tossed in sugar. Sprinkle with the kirsch or orange juice and serve with or without cream.

(4–6 portions)

Vegetables and Salads

75. QUICKIE SALAD

A salad that is quickly made and eaten, when served with cold meat.

INGREDIENTS

- ½ lb. home grown English tomatoes (Blues)
- 2 oz. cup mushrooms
- 4 oz. cooked home grown peas
- 1 oz. finely chopped parsley
- Lemon and oil dressing – 1 part lemon to 3 parts salad oil

METHOD: Pour boiling water over the tomatoes and skin them. Then slice the tomatoes and mushrooms, and put into a serving dish. Pour the dressing over and allow this to soak through before adding the parsley and peas. Toss all ingredients well together and serve. (4 portions)

76. HOT POTATO SALAD

This is an ideal salad to have with hot fish, meat, poultry or sausages. It is also an excellent accompaniment to a plate of cold meat, ham or bacon.

INGREDIENTS

- 1 lb. home grown new potatoes
- 4 tablespoonsful chutney or relish
- 4 tablespoonsful salad dressing
- 1 tablespoonful vinegar
- Salt and pepper to taste

METHOD: Boil the potatoes, skin and cut into dice. Then put all the ingredients into a saucepan and warm through gently.

(3–4 portions)

77. VEGETABLE HOT-POT

A dish for the vegetarian, or those wishing to have a change from meat.

INGREDIENTS

- 2 large potatoes (peeled and sliced)
- 2 large carrots (cleaned and sliced)
- 2 sticks celery (cleaned and sliced)
- 1 large onion (peeled and sliced)
- 8-oz. can baked beans in tomato sauce
- ½ pint hot water
- 1 small level teaspoonful Marmite
- Pepper to taste
- 1–2 oz. grated Cheddar cheese
- ½ oz. margarine

METHOD: Melt the margarine in a frying pan and cook the onion (which has been pressed out into rings) until golden brown. Into a 2-pint ovenproof dish put half the potatoes, continue in layers with the carrots, celery and onion. Then add the baked beans, season to taste, and put the remaining potatoes in a layer on the top. Mix the Marmite with the hot water and pour over, cover with a lid and cook at approximately 400° F or mark 7 for 1–2 hours depending on the thickness of the sliced vegetables. Once the vegetables are tender sprinkle the grated cheese all over the top and leave in the oven until it has melted. Serve very hot with a green vegetable.

(3–4 portions)

78. EGG AND VEGETABLE SCRAMBLE

This dish can be varied by adding any vegetables you happen to have handy at the time.

INGREDIENTS

2 oz. butter
3 oz. mushrooms (quartered)
3 tomatoes (peeled and quartered)
¼ lb. cooked peas
5–6 oz. cooked diced potatoes
4 large eggs
Salt and pepper to taste
Little grated cheese (optional)

METHOD: Melt the butter in a frying pan, add the potatoes and mushrooms and cook 1–2 minutes, then add the tomatoes and peas. When they are thoroughly heated through add 4 lightly beaten eggs, pouring them all over the vegetables, and season to taste. Finally add a little grated cheese and cook slowly with a lid or plate over the top until the eggs are set, about 10 minutes. Serve hot from the pan or on a hot serving dish.

(4 portions)

79. STUFFED POTATOES

A tasty dish for hungry youngsters.

INGREDIENTS

2 large potatoes (well scrubbed)
4 oz. cooked and minced chicken, turkey, goose, duck or ham
2 oz. grated Cheddar cheese
Few drops Worcester sauce
1 oz. butter
Milk to mix
Salt and pepper to taste

METHOD: Wrap each potato in foil, place these on the shelf of the oven and cook until tender when pressed with the fingers, at approximately 450° F or mark 8. When cooked slice the potatoes in half lengthwise, and scoop out the cooked potato into a basin, reserving the skins and foil. Make the foil into boat shapes to hold the skins and place them in.

Add to the potato the minced meat, half the grated cheese, sauce and butter, add enough milk to give a fluffy consistency and season to taste.

Divide the mixture between the potato shells, sprinkle on the remaining cheese, pop back into the oven to heat through and serve with cranberry sauce.

(2–4 portions)

80. ASPARAGUS WITH MINT

When cooked properly asparagus is delicious, but overcooking destroys its flavour.

INGREDIENTS

1 bundle Evesham asparagus
1 sprig mint
Salted boiling water
Melted butter

METHOD: Scrape the butt ends of the asparagus. Tie in one portion bundles with thin string or cotton. Put the bundles into a large pan of boiling salted water, add the mint, cover with a lid and cook for about 15–20 minutes, depending on the size of the sticks. Drain on a clean cloth, untie the bundles and serve with lots of melted butter. (3 portions)

81. AVOCADO PEARS WITH PRAWNS OR SHRIMPS

The taste of a ripe avocado pear is one to be remembered, Here are two ways of serving them.

INGREDIENTS

2 Israel avocado pears
5 oz. fresh prawns or shrimps
or
8-oz. can of prawns or shrimps (well drained)
Few drops lemon juice
1 sieved hard boiled egg
Little chopped parsley or chives
2 level tablespoonsful mayonnaise
Salt and pepper to taste

METHOD: Halve the pears and remove seed. In a basin mix together the mayonnaise, prawns or shrimps (saving a few for decoration), lemon juice and seasoning to taste. Fill the cavities in the pears with thc filling and top with sieved hard boiled egg. Decorate with the remaining prawns or shrimps, and parsley or chives. Serve chilled. (4 portions)

82. AVOCADO WITH FRIED BACON

INGREDIENTS

1 Israel avocado pear
Few drops lemon juice
Salt to taste
1–2 drops tabasco sauce
1 rasher fried streaky bacon

METHOD: In a basin mash the pear until creamy with a fork, add lemon juice, salt and sauce, and mix all well together. Cut the bacon into small dice and place it in an individual dish, leaving one or two pieces for garnish. Pile the creamed avocado pear on top and garnish with the remaining bacon. Serve well chilled. (1 portion)

Picnics and Parties

83. TORTA DELL 'ADRIATICO

Three dishes which are eaten on the Adriatic coast of Italy, but can also be made and eaten in this country.

INGREDIENTS

- 4 cooked pancakes approximately 6" diameter
- 8 oz. Russian salad
- $6\frac{1}{2}$ oz. tunny fish (flaked)
- 2 oz. anchovies (chopped)
- 6 olives (sliced)
- 12 capers
- 5 oz. prawns (drained weight)
- 1 hard boiled egg
- Few drops fresh lemon juice

METHOD: Put a cold pancake on to a serving dish, then spread half the Russian salad over the surface. On top of this put the tunny fish, anchovies, olives, capers, most of the prawns and half of the hard boiled egg which has been chopped, mixing them all well together in a basin, and lastly adding the lemon juice and seasoning to taste. Once this has been spread all over the surface cover with another pancake and cut into 4 portions. Continue with the other pancakes in the same way. To serve garnish each wedge with a prawn and a wedge of hard boiled egg. (8 portions)

84. ESCALOPE OF VEAL MODENESE

INGREDIENTS

1 escalope of veal
Beaten egg and breadcrumbs for coating
Oil for frying
1 thin slice of ham
1 thin slice Gruyère cheese

METHOD: Dip the veal in the egg and coat with breadcrumbs. Heat the oil in a frying pan and cook the veal until tender. When cooked place on a heatproof dish, cover with the ham and finally the cheese and place under the grill until the cheese melts. Serve at once. (1 portion)

85. CRÈME EXPRESSO

INGREDIENTS

6 oz. top quality cream cheese
2 egg yolks
2½ oz. castor sugar
2 fluid oz. medium strength coffee
2 sponge cakes (cut into quarters)

METHOD: In a basin beat together for about 10 minutes the cheese, egg yolks, sugar and coffee. Into individual dishes place a piece of sponge cake, pour the cream equally between the dishes and stand in a cold place. Serve cold. (4–6 portions)

86. PICNIC SALAD

Here is a picnic dish, but if the weather should change it can be eaten at home.

INGREDIENTS

Potato Salad

1 lb. home grown new potatoes
¼ pint mayonnaise or salad cream
Salt and pepper
Few chopped chives or spring onions

Accompaniments

½ lb. sausages
Few rashers of streaky bacon
4 tomatoes
Small quantity of cooked garden peas
1 small lettuce

METHOD: Boil the potatoes in their skins, and while still hot remove the skins and cut the potatoes into small dice. Mix gently with the mayonnaise or salad cream. Season to taste and add the chopped chives or onions. Wrap one rasher of bacon round each of the sausages and grill until cooked. Assemble all the ingredients on foil trays, cover and they are ready to take on the picnic. (4 portions)

87. CHEESE AND WALNUT CREAMS

A recipe for party times, particularly good when accompanied by a drink.

INGREDIENTS

- 5-oz. carton cottage cheese
- 1 large piece crystallised ginger
- Approximately 60 walnut halves
- Waxed sweet cases

METHOD: Rub the cottage cheese through a fine sieve, add the finely chopped ginger and mix well together. Sandwich the walnut halves together with the mixture and put into the sweet cases. (Approximately 30)

88. SALAD PICNIC LOAF

Going out for the day? Why not try this picnic loaf?

INGREDIENTS

- 2 small French loaves
- 4 slices of ham, tongue or bacon
- 4 tablespoonsful cabbage (very finely shredded)
- 2 tablespoonsful finely diced cucumber
- 2 tablespoonsful mayonnaise
- 2 tablespoonsful double cream (whipped)
- 1 dessertspoonful chopped walnuts
- 3 oz. fresh mushrooms (chopped)
- Few drops lemon juice

METHOD: In a basin mix the cabbage, cucumber, mushrooms and nuts, and sprinkle with a few drops of lemon juice. Stir the cream and mayonnaise together, pour over the other ingredients and turn the salad over to blend thoroughly. Stand in a cool place for 15–20 minutes. Cut the loaves almost through, remove a little of the crumb, lay the slices of meat in the base of the loaf, and fill with the salad.

89. TOASTED SANDWICHES

When unexpected guests arrive, these make a tasty snack.

Make the sandwiches in the usual way with either brown or white bread, but once they are filled lightly spread the outside of the sandwiches with butter. Once they are all done toast on both sides under a hot grill, and when done remove the crusts before serving very hot.

Suggested Fillings

1. One 7-oz. can of chopped pork with ham, cut in slices and spread with a little mustard.
2. Grated Cheddar cheese mixed with pickle or chutney.
3. Small tin salmon, mixed with mayonnaise or sandwich spread.

These sandwiches will be delicious providing the filling is moist enough to allow the heat to penetrate, and the combination of ingredients blend well together.

90. STUFFED GRAPES

This recipe was given to me by a friend of the family.

INGREDIENTS

20 Belgian large black grapes   2 oz. cream cheese

METHOD: Cut the grapes in half and remove the seeds. Spread some cream cheese on to one half and top with another half. Secure through the centre of the grape with a cocktail stick and continue with the other grapes. Serve chilled. (20 portions)

91. MEAL IN A SANDWICH

A quickly made sandwich, that will keep you going if time is at a premium.

Lightly toast 3 slices of brown or white bread, remove the crusts and butter two on one side and the third on both sides, as it goes in the middle of the sandwich. On the first slice spread cooked cold chicken which has been mixed with mayonnaise and a few chopped, blanched almonds.

Cover with the centre slice of toast and put on top, lettuce, sliced tomato and two slices of grilled bacon, top with the third slice buttered side down. Cut in half diagonally, and put a cocktail stick through the middle of each half.

Serve at once.

92. SANDWICH LOAF

This loaf can be taken on a picnic or served at a party.

INGREDIENTS

1 small sandwich loaf (day old if possible)

Fillings suggested

1. Soften 3 oz. cream cheese, adding a little milk if necessary, add 3 finely sliced spring onions.
2. Mix 2 dessertspoonsful mayonnaise with 2 finely chopped hard boiled eggs, 4 chopped stuffed olives, and ½ tomato or small piece of pimento.
3. Whip 2 oz. double cream, add 1 oz. blanched and chopped almonds, and 2 oz. diced ham or chicken.

Approximately 9 oz. of cream cheese is required to coat the loaf when finished.

METHOD: Trim all the crusts from the loaf and make a uniform shape. Cut the loaf lengthwise into 4 pieces of equal thickness.

Lightly butter the layers and put one filling between each layer of bread. If desired the top and sides can be coated with cream cheese of a spreading consistency; it can be coloured (perhaps for a party) and decorated with slices of stuffed olives and gherkin fans.

N.B. There are many other fillings suitable for this particular dish.

Drinks

93. CIDER CUP

A refreshing drink with an orange flavour.

INGREDIENTS:

- ½ tumbler dry cider
- 2 tablespoonsful fresh orange juice
- 1 teaspoonful fresh lemon juice
- 1 tablespoonful orange liqueur (Cointreau)
- 1 split-size bottle soda water

METHOD: Chill the cider, lemon and orange juice. Just before serving measure out the cider, add fruit juices, liqueur and mix well together. Add the soda water to the top of the glass, pour into 2 glasses and decorate with a cocktail cherry and orange and lemon slices. Serve at once. (2 drinks)

94. OLD FASHIONED COCKTAIL

A drink with a kick! Adaptable to most spirits.

INGREDIENTS

1 tot of whisky, rum, gin or brandy
4 drops aromatic bitters (angostura bitters)
1 teaspoonful sugar syrup
1 tot cold water

METHOD: Into a glass put the spirit selected by you, add the bitters and syrup and finally the water, stir them all well together, and serve at once. If liked the drink can be mixed with a few ice cubes and then strained into the glass. (1 glass)

95. CARNIVAL COOLIES

A really cold refreshing drink. A great favourite with children.

INGREDIENTS

1 pint cold milk
1 family brick chocolate carnival or ripple ice cream
Little grated chocolate

METHOD: Pour the milk into a basin, cut the ice cream into small pieces and add to the milk. Whisk all well together until evenly blended. Pour into the glasses and sprinkle the top of each glass with the chocolate. Serve with a swizzle stick or spoon if the drink is allowed to stand. (4 drinks)

96. HIGHLAND TEA

An unusual recipe using cold tea – it really tastes better than it sounds.

INGREDIENTS

1 measure of double strength tea (cold)
1 measure Scotch whisky
½ measure strained lemon juice
Castor sugar to taste (approximately 1 teaspoonful)
Small quantity dry ginger
Few ice cubes

METHOD: Mix tea, whisky and lemon juice together, and add sugar to taste. Stir all well together then quarter fill a tumbler with ice cubes. Add the other liquids and top up with dry ginger.

(1 glass)

97. CHOCOLATE CARAMEL CREAM

A rich, but also delicious milk drink.

INGREDIENTS

1 pint milk
2 oz. chocolate coated caramels
1 standard egg yolk
¼ pint double cream

METHOD: Into a saucepan put the milk and caramels, and warm together over a very low heat, until the caramels have melted, stirring occasionally. When melted pour the liquid on to the beaten egg yolk, stir until evenly blended, and set aside to chill, thoroughly. Lightly whip the cream and stir into the chilled mixture just before serving. Serve in tumblers, using straws if liked.

(3 drinks)

98. EIGHTEENTH-CENTURY MULLED WINE

This worked out at approximately 1s. per glass and I used British ruby wine from the cask.

INGREDIENTS

1 bottle red ruby wine
12–15 lumps of sugar
6 cloves
1 pint boiling water
1 wine glass orange curaçao
1 wine glass brandy
Little grated nutmeg

METHOD: Into a saucepan put the wine, cloves and sugar, bring almost to the boil. Add the boiling water, curaçao and brandy. Pour directly into heatproof glasses or mugs and sprinkle a little nutmeg on top. Serve at once.

(Approximately 10 glasses)

99. REFRESHING CIDER CUP

A refreshing drink for parties or during the summer months.

INGREDIENTS

1 pint sparkling cider
1 oz. castor sugar
½ lemon (sliced)
½ orange (sliced)
1 bottle soda water (split)
1 small glass brandy

METHOD: Cut the lemon and orange into thin slices, and place in a glass serving bowl. Sprinkle on the castor sugar and allow to stand for 5–10 minutes. Next pour on the brandy and cider, and allow to stand for about 1 hour in a cool place or the refrigerator, but it must be covered. Just before serving add the soda water, which has been well chilled. Serve at once.

100. CHAMPAGNE COCKTAIL

A good brand of non-vintage champagne is excellent for this cocktail and this compares favourably in price with most other cocktails.

INGREDIENTS

1 bottle champagne
6–8 small lumps sugar
6–8 thimblefuls brandy
Angostura bitters
6–8 small slices fresh orange

METHOD: Ice the champagne well. Into each glass put a small lump of sugar, a thimbleful of brandy and a dash of angostura bitters. Just before serving pour in the champagne, and add a small slice of orange. (6–8 glasses)

Index